HOW THE WORLD WORKS
AN OXFAM GUIDE

Written by **David Thorpe**

Illustrated by **Aidan Potts**

TWO-CAN

CONTENTS

Words in **bold** appear in the glossary

RICH WORLD POOR WORLD

BEFORE YOU CAN UNDERSTAND HOW THE WORLD WORKS, YOU NEED TO KNOW WHY THINGS ARE THE WAY THEY ARE. ARE YOU RICH, ANYA?

YOU MUST BE JOKING! BUT I'M NOT REALLY POOR, EITHER.

JUST LIKE PEOPLE, THERE ARE SOME POOR COUNTRIES...

...AND SOME RICH COUNTRIES.

THE POOR COUNTRIES ARE POOR IN MONEY BUT RICH IN MANY OTHER THINGS. THEY HAVE MOST OF THE WORLD'S **NATURAL RESOURCES** SUCH AS GOLD, OIL, COAL OR IRON AND LOTS OF LAND, AND BEST OF ALL, LOTS OF PEOPLE.

WHAT THEY NEED IS MONEY TO HELP MAKE THE BEST USE OF THESE RESOURCES.

IT WASN'T ALWAYS LIKE IT IS NOW...

NORTH AMERICA

EUROPE

SOUTH AMERICA

AFRICA

INDIA

THE FAR EAST

☐ PARTS OF THE WORLD CONQUERED BY EUROPEAN EXPLORERS IN THE 15TH AND 16TH CENTURIES.

For most of history, people around the world had more or less enough to eat and drink. Barring the odd **natural disaster** such as earthquakes, they survived, though often they didn't live long.

Empires rose and fell around the world, but what happened in one part of the world had little effect on people in other places.

About 500 years ago people from Europe started to explore the world. They sailed to the Americas, Africa, India and the Far East.

Although people already lived there, the Europeans thought they'd discovered these nations. They conquered them and began using their natural resources.

These nations became the **colonies** of European countries like England, Holland, Spain and Portugal.

Nowadays most of these countries rule themselves. But they still tend to sell their **raw materials** to the countries of the **North** which used to control them, and buy most of their **manufactured goods** from them, too.

THE COUNTRIES OF THE NORTH WANT TO PAY AS LITTLE AS POSSIBLE FOR THE GOODS THEY BUY, BUT THE COUNTRIES OF THE **SOUTH** NEED TO MAKE AS MUCH MONEY AS THEY CAN.

WHAT THE POOR COUNTRIES NEED IS FAIRER **TRADE**.

TRADE AND MONEY

POOR COUNTRIES NEED MONEY TO PAY FOR NEW HOMES, FACTORIES, BUILDINGS, SCHOOLS AND EQUIPMENT.

LIKE GOVERNMENTS EVERYWHERE, THE GOVERNMENTS OF THE COUNTRIES IN THE SOUTH DON'T ALWAYS MAKE THE BEST DECISIONS FOR THEIR PEOPLE.

MY MUM SAYS THAT INDIA, WHERE SHE CAME FROM, SPENDS MONEY BUILDING SPACE ROCKETS AND NUCLEAR POWER STATIONS BUT STILL THERE ARE TEN MILLION PEOPLE WHO DON'T GET ENOUGH TO EAT. SHE SAYS THAT PEOPLE IN INDIA WORK VERY HARD TO SURVIVE.

HOW MUCH IS YOUR COFFEE?

IT'S £20 A SACK.

I'LL GIVE YOU £15.

ONLY £15 — AFTER ALL MY HARD WORK! THAT'S THE THIRD TIME THIS YEAR YOU'VE LOWERED THE PRICE. HOW AM I EXPECTED TO SURVIVE?

PEOPLE ALL OVER THE WORLD WORK HARD. BUT MUCH OF WHAT WE GROW OR MAKE IN THE SOUTH IS SOLD TO THE NORTH— AND THE NORTH DOESN'T PAY A FAIR PRICE.

YOU COULD SAY THE NORTH MAKES THE RULES AND THE SOUTH HAS TO PLAY BY THEM.

I COULD LEND YOU SOME MONEY. MY INTEREST RATE IS VERY REASONABLE.

WHAT ELSE CAN I DO? I NEED MONEY **NOW**. PAYING BACK THE MONEY WE'VE BORROWED COSTS MY COUNTRY ABOUT A QUARTER OF WHAT WE MAKE SELLING OUR GOODS TO THE NORTH.

SO THE SOUTH NEEDS MORE MONEY ... BUT WHERE CAN THEY GET IT FROM? THE RICH COUNTRIES OF THE NORTH?

IT OFTEN SEEMS LIKE THE NORTH IS ALWAYS GIVING MONEY TO THE SOUTH— WHEN THERE'S A **FAMINE** OR A FLOOD, FOR EXAMPLE.

ACTUALLY, EACH YEAR THE POOR COUNTRIES PAY BACK A LOT MORE TO THE NORTH THAN THEY GET FRO THE NORTH IN **AID** A NEW LOANS. BUT WHAT WE PAY WILL NEVER BE ENOUGH OUR DEBT TO THE RICH COUNTRIES IS JUST TOO BIG.

BORROWING AND LENDING

SO SOUTHERN COUNTRIES MUST HAVE LESS TO SPEND ON SCHOOLS, FOOD AND HOUSES, LET ALONE TELEVISIONS, CARS AND VIDEOS...

MONEY EARNED EVERY YEAR FROM SELLING GOODS TO THE NORTH

AMOUNT LEFT TO PAY FOR RUNNING SOUTHERN COUNTRIES (eg. FOR FOOD, FUEL, HOUSES, WATER SUPPLIES, ROADS, SCHOOLS, EQUIPMENT AND OTHER GOODS).

AMOUNT SPENT ON REPAYING DEBT TO THE NORTH.

WHEN IT GETS TO THE NORTH, ALL THAT MONEY FROM THE POOR COUNTRIES GOES STRAIGHT TO THE BANKS.

BIG BANK INC.

¥ $ £   CASH

MY COUNTRY NEEDS TO BORROW MONEY— BUT ON FAIR TERMS. WHEN WE FIRST BORROWED MONEY, THE INTEREST RATES WERE LOWER THAN NOW. THEN THE WORLD'S ECONOMY SLOWED DOWN AND INTEREST RATES WENT UP.

SOME OF THE BANKS AND GOVERNMENTS IN THE SOUTH HAVE MADE BAD DECISIONS TOO. BUT WHATEVER THE CAUSE, IT'S ORDINARY PEOPLE LIKE US WHO HAVE TO SUFFER THE RESULTS.

YES IT'S PEOPLE LIKE YOU AND ME WHO SHOULD ENCOURAGE BANKS AND GOVERNMENTS IN THE NORTH TO HELP COUNTRIES IN THE SOUTH.

FOOD AND FARMING

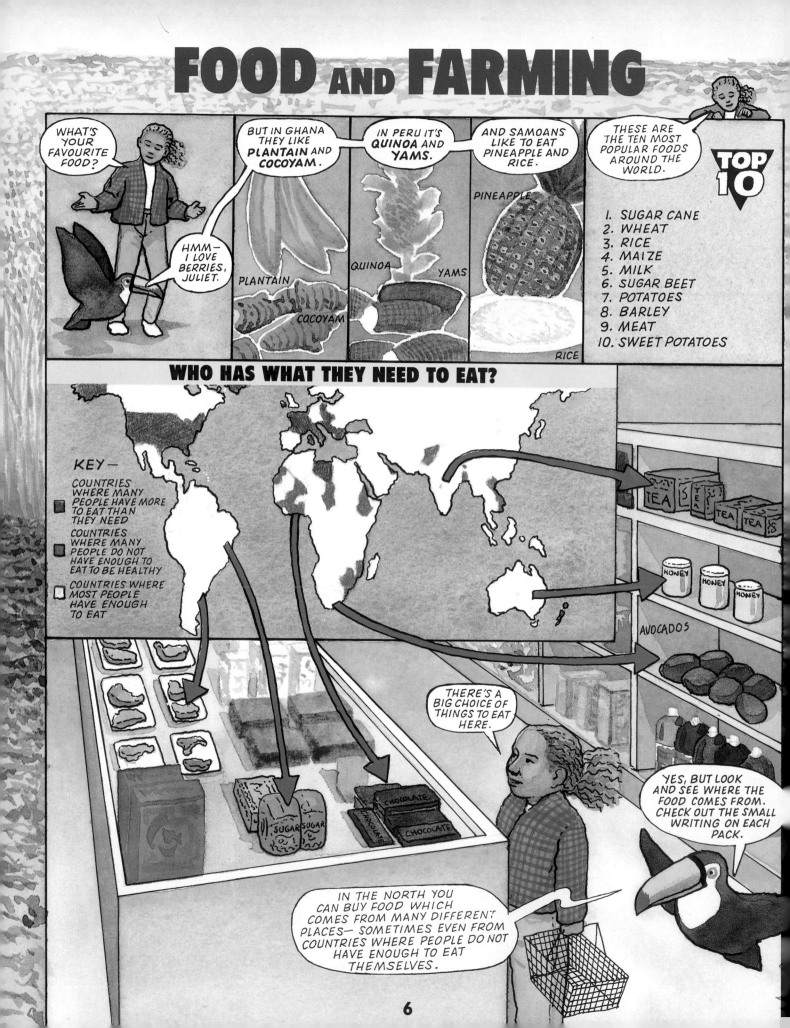

FOOD AROUND THE WORLD

WE NEED VEGETABLES NOT GRAIN.

I'VE HEARD THERE'S NOT ENOUGH FOOD TO FEED EVERYONE IN THE WORLD.

WITHOUT A ROAD I CAN'T DELIVER THESE SUPPLIES.

THEY COST A WEEK'S WAGES!

WELL THERE IS — BUT IT'S OFTEN NOT THE RIGHT FOOD —

— OR IN THE RIGHT PLACE —

— OR AT THE RIGHT PRICE.

INDIA

PERU

CAMBODIA

THERE ARE LOTS OF FARMS IN THE SOUTH.

DIFFERENT PLANTS LIKE DIFFERENT SOILS, DIFFERENT TEMPERATURES AND DIFFERENT RAINFALL SO THEY GROW IN DIFFERENT PLACES IN THE WORLD. THE PROBLEM IS PARTLY GROWING ENOUGH FOOD, PARTLY GROWING THE RIGHT KIND AND PARTLY GETTING IT TO THE PEOPLE WHO NEED IT.

BURKINA FASO

BURKINA FASO

WHY FOOD DOESN'T GET WHERE IT'S NEEDED

DROUGHT

LOW WAGES

MY FAMILY CAN'T LIVE ON THIS!

BAD ADVICE

I WAS TOLD TO PLANT AT THE WRONG TIME!

CONFLICT

THIS WAR! IT REALLY MESSES UP OUR LIVES!

CORRUPTION

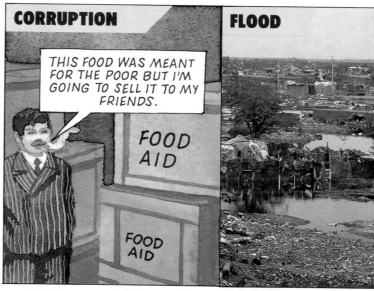

THIS FOOD WAS MEANT FOR THE POOR BUT I'M GOING TO SELL IT TO MY FRIENDS.

FOOD AID

FOOD AID

FLOOD

NO ROADS, FUEL OR TRANSPORTATION

HOW CAN I TAKE THIS WHERE IT'S NEEDED?

FARMERS NOT ALLOWED TO USE LAND

PRIVATE KEEP OUT!

HOW CAN I FARM WITHOUT LAND?

CASH CROPS

ALL THE GOOD LAND'S BEEN USED TO GROW CROPS TO SELL ABROAD.

CASH CROPS

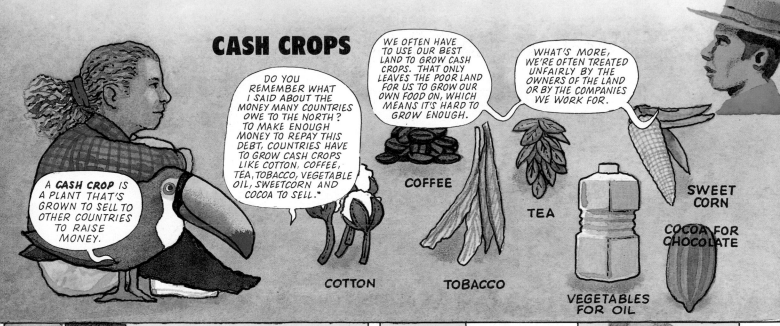

A **CASH CROP** IS A PLANT THAT'S GROWN TO SELL TO OTHER COUNTRIES TO RAISE MONEY.

DO YOU REMEMBER WHAT I SAID ABOUT THE MONEY MANY COUNTRIES OWE TO THE NORTH? TO MAKE ENOUGH MONEY TO REPAY THIS DEBT, COUNTRIES HAVE TO GROW CASH CROPS LIKE COTTON, COFFEE, TEA, TOBACCO, VEGETABLE OIL, SWEETCORN AND COCOA TO SELL."

WE OFTEN HAVE TO USE OUR BEST LAND TO GROW CASH CROPS. THAT ONLY LEAVES THE POOR LAND FOR US TO GROW OUR OWN FOOD ON, WHICH MEANS IT'S HARD TO GROW ENOUGH.

WHAT'S MORE, WE'RE OFTEN TREATED UNFAIRLY BY THE OWNERS OF THE LAND OR BY THE COMPANIES WE WORK FOR.

COFFEE

COTTON

TEA

TOBACCO

SWEET CORN

VEGETABLES FOR OIL

COCOA FOR CHOCOLATE

I'LL PAY YOU £55 FOR THE LOAD AND I'LL CHARGE £20 FOR THE LORRY RIDE TO MARKET AND £30 RENT FOR THE LAND YOU GROW YOUR CROPS ON.

SO THAT LEAVES £5. OK?

BUT I NEED £20 TO LIVE ON!

TOO BAD. THAT'S MY PRICE. TAKE IT OR LEAVE IT.

THE STORY OF CHOCOLATE

DID YOU KNOW THAT CHOCOLATE COMES FROM THE CACAO OR COCOA PLANT? ORIGINALLY IT CAME FROM CENTRAL AMERICA AND THE BEANS WERE WORSHIPPED AS DIVINE FOOD FOR THE BIRD-GOD QUETZALCOATL.

WHEN THE EUROPEANS DISCOVERED COCOA IT BECAME VERY TRENDY AND THEY MADE FARMERS IN WEST AFRICA GROW NOTHING ELSE.

I'VE NEVER EATEN CHOCOLATE MYSELF. ALTHOUGH I GROW THE BEANS, IT'S NOT EASY TO BUY CHOCO-LATE BARS ON THE PLANT-ATION, BUT THEY ARE ON SALE IN THE TOWN.

COCOA IS MUCH CHEAPER THAN IT USED TO BE, SO I'M WORSE OFF NOW.

HALF MY COUNTRY'S CHILDREN ARE GOING HUNGRY WHILE WE USE THE LAND TO GROW COCOA AS A CASH CROP INSTEAD OF FOOD FOR OURSELVES. AND SOME-WHERE IN THE WORLD THERE'S A HUGE COCOA MOUNTAIN THAT CAN'T BE SOLD.

WONDER WHERE IT IS...?

NOW THAT THE LAND IS MINE, I DON'T HAVE TO PAY **RENT** TO THE LANDLORD.

THE SITUATION COULD BE IMPROVED FOR FARMERS IN THE SOUTH. HERE ARE SOME OF THE THINGS THAT WOULD MAKE LIFE FAIRER THERE...

MAKES YOU THINK

• Helping small farmers to own the land they work on.

• Providing tractors and equipment but also encouraging traditional farming methods.

• Helping farmers to get their crops to market and get a fair price.

• Giving seeds and tools direct to small local groups, especially to the women, who do much of the farm work.

• Listening to local people — they often know what works best.

• Working for democracy so people can change bad governments.

• Cancelling the debts owed by the poor countries to the rich ones.

• Paying Southern countries a fair price for their goods.

• Encouraging governments to spend money on developing roads, water supplies, better ways of growing food etc, not on weapons.

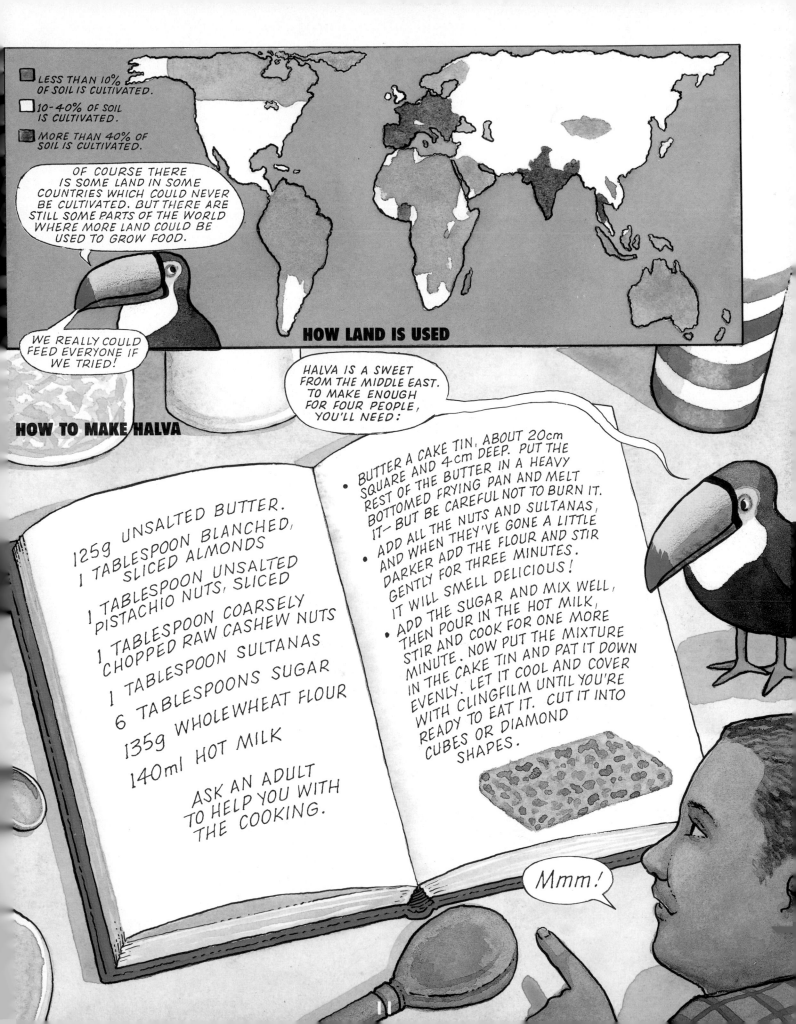

HOW LAND IS USED

LESS THAN 10% OF SOIL IS CULTIVATED.

10-40% OF SOIL IS CULTIVATED.

MORE THAN 40% OF SOIL IS CULTIVATED.

OF COURSE THERE IS SOME LAND IN SOME COUNTRIES WHICH COULD NEVER BE CULTIVATED. BUT THERE ARE STILL SOME PARTS OF THE WORLD WHERE MORE LAND COULD BE USED TO GROW FOOD.

WE REALLY COULD FEED EVERYONE IF WE TRIED!

HOW TO MAKE HALVA

HALVA IS A SWEET FROM THE MIDDLE EAST. TO MAKE ENOUGH FOR FOUR PEOPLE, YOU'LL NEED:

125g UNSALTED BUTTER.

1 TABLESPOON BLANCHED, SLICED ALMONDS

1 TABLESPOON UNSALTED PISTACHIO NUTS, SLICED

1 TABLESPOON COARSELY CHOPPED RAW CASHEW NUTS

1 TABLESPOON SULTANAS

6 TABLESPOONS SUGAR

135g WHOLEWHEAT FLOUR

140ml HOT MILK

ASK AN ADULT TO HELP YOU WITH THE COOKING.

- BUTTER A CAKE TIN, ABOUT 20cm SQUARE AND 4cm DEEP. PUT THE REST OF THE BUTTER IN A HEAVY BOTTOMED FRYING PAN AND MELT IT— BUT BE CAREFUL NOT TO BURN IT.

- ADD ALL THE NUTS AND SULTANAS, AND WHEN THEY'VE GONE A LITTLE DARKER ADD THE FLOUR AND STIR GENTLY FOR THREE MINUTES. IT WILL SMELL DELICIOUS!

- ADD THE SUGAR AND MIX WELL, THEN POUR IN THE HOT MILK, STIR AND COOK FOR ONE MORE MINUTE. NOW PUT THE MIXTURE IN THE CAKE TIN AND PAT IT DOWN EVENLY. LET IT COOL AND COVER WITH CLINGFILM UNTIL YOU'RE READY TO EAT IT. CUT IT INTO CUBES OR DIAMOND SHAPES.

Mmm!

WATER

I'M THIRSTY. I'M GOING TO GET A GLASS OF WATER.

YOU KNOW LI, MANY PEOPLE CAN'T GET CLEAN WATER IF THEY'RE THIRSTY. HAVE YOU EVER THOUGHT HOW LUCKY YOU ARE TO HAVE IT ON TAP? PEOPLE IN MORE THAN HALF THE HOUSEHOLDS IN THE WORLD HAVE TO WALK UP TO 6 OR 7 KILOMETRES TO THE NEAREST RIVER, TAP OR PUMP TO FETCH ALL THE WATER THEY USE.

MALI

20 KILOS.

IT MUST TAKE HOURS AND I BET IT'S REALLY HEAVY.

KENYA

WE ALL NEED WATER TO DRINK, COOK WITH AND WASH.

PLACES WHERE PEOPLE CAN'T GET CLEAN WATER CLOSE TO HOME

KEY:

☐ BAD— LESS THAN 20% HAVE CLEAN WATER

☐ GOOD— OVER 75% HAVE CLEAN WATER

WATER IS IMPORTANT FOR KEEPING US HEALTHY, TOO.

TO JUDGE THE HEALTH OF A NATION DON'T COUNT THE HOSPITAL BEDS - COUNT THE WATER PUMPS.

World Health Organisation.

HUMAN BEINGS ARE 7/10 WATER! THEY NEED TO DRINK AT LEAST 3 LITRES A DAY!

THE PROBLEM: Disease and Floods

THIS IS WHAT HAPPENS IF A WELL GETS INFECTED BY PEOPLE, INSECTS OR FLOODS.

FOUR OUT OF FIVE ILLNESSES IN THE WORLD WOULD DISAPPEAR IF EVERYONE HAD SAFE WATER.

THAT'S A LOT!

BUT WHAT MAKES THINGS LIKE FLOODS AND DROUGHTS HAPPEN, APART FROM RAIN?

NOT JUST BAD WEATHER—IT'S HOW PEOPLE TREAT THE LAND. THIS WOMAN NEEDS FIREWOOD, SO SHE HAS TO CHOP DOWN TREES.

I NEED FIREWOOD!

WHEN IT RAINS THERE ARE NO ROOTS TO HOLD THE SOIL TOGETHER AND SOAK UP THE WATER.

SO THE WATER RUNS DOWN THE HILLSIDE AND FLOODS THE LAND BELOW.

NEW TREES SHOULD BE PLANTED WHEN FIREWOOD IS COLLECTED!

THE SOLUTION: Taps and Pumps

BEFORE THE PUMP

THE WELL HAS DRIED UP!

EVERYBODY SHOULD HAVE A CLEAN WELL OR PUMP.

AFTER THE PUMP

MOZAMBIQUE

13

WATER IN THE CITIES

MAKES YOU THINK

USUALLY ALL THAT'S NEEDED IS MONEY TO SUPPLY PUMPS, PIPES AND TAPS— THE PEOPLE LIVING IN THE AREA CAN INSTALL AND MAINTAIN THEM.

THINGS TO DO

JUST THINK ABOUT HOW MUCH WATER YOU USE EACH DAY— INCLUDING FLUSHING THE TOILET AND WASHING UP.

I NEVER REALISED IT WAS SO MUCH!

SEE HOW HEAVY 3 LITRES IS. CAN YOU LIFT IT? HOW FAR CAN YOU CARRY IT? (BE CAREFUL).

IT WEIGHS 3 KILOS. THAT'S REALLY HEAVY.

SEE IF YOU CAN MANAGE USING ONLY 5 LITRES OF WATER IN A DAY—FOR DRINKING, WASHING UP AND FLUSHING THE TOILET.

DIFFICULT— BUT POSSIBLE. TAKING A SHOWER USES MUCH LESS WATER THAN A BATH, BUT I'LL PROBABLY STILL NEED MORE THAN 5 LITRES.

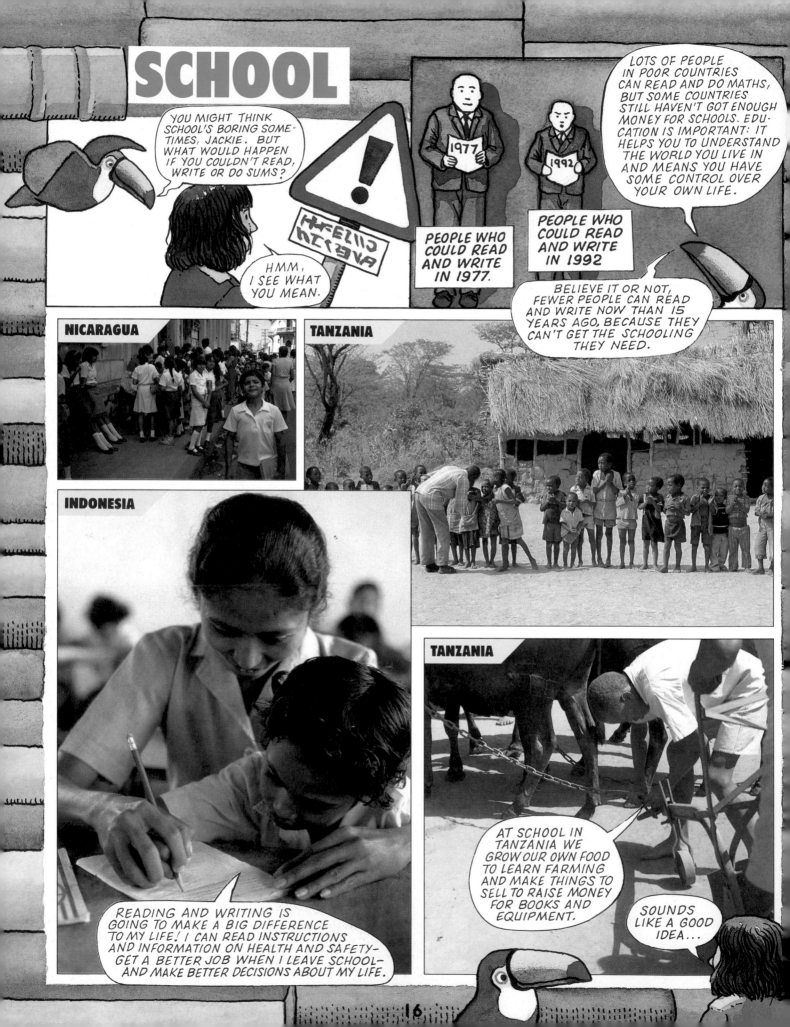

SCHOOL

YOU MIGHT THINK SCHOOL'S BORING SOMETIMES, JACKIE. BUT WHAT WOULD HAPPEN IF YOU COULDN'T READ, WRITE OR DO SUMS?

HMM, I SEE WHAT YOU MEAN.

LOTS OF PEOPLE IN POOR COUNTRIES CAN READ AND DO MATHS, BUT SOME COUNTRIES STILL HAVEN'T GOT ENOUGH MONEY FOR SCHOOLS. EDUCATION IS IMPORTANT: IT HELPS YOU TO UNDERSTAND THE WORLD YOU LIVE IN AND MEANS YOU HAVE SOME CONTROL OVER YOUR OWN LIFE.

PEOPLE WHO COULD READ AND WRITE IN 1977.

PEOPLE WHO COULD READ AND WRITE IN 1992

BELIEVE IT OR NOT, FEWER PEOPLE CAN READ AND WRITE NOW THAN 15 YEARS AGO, BECAUSE THEY CAN'T GET THE SCHOOLING THEY NEED.

NICARAGUA

TANZANIA

INDONESIA

TANZANIA

READING AND WRITING IS GOING TO MAKE A BIG DIFFERENCE TO MY LIFE! I CAN READ INSTRUCTIONS AND INFORMATION ON HEALTH AND SAFETY-GET A BETTER JOB WHEN I LEAVE SCHOOL-AND MAKE BETTER DECISIONS ABOUT MY LIFE.

AT SCHOOL IN TANZANIA WE GROW OUR OWN FOOD TO LEARN FARMING AND MAKE THINGS TO SELL TO RAISE MONEY FOR BOOKS AND EQUIPMENT.

SOUNDS LIKE A GOOD IDEA...

JOSEPH'S TIMETABLE

JOSEPH GOES TO A SECONDARY SCHOOL IN ZIMBABWE, A COUNTRY IN SOUTHERN AFRICA.

5.15am: Get up, put on my smart school clothes and walk 5 kilometres to school.

7.00am: Assembly outside in the fresh air. We sing songs about our nation.

7.30am: Lessons begin — there are about 50 pupils to a classroom. We share desks and books. Our headmaster sometimes has to cut up exercise books to make enough to go round. We learn reading, writing, social studies, maths, geography and science. And, of course, our own language — Shona or Ndebele.

11.30am: Lunch break. But many of us can't afford anything to eat. I walk the 10 kilometres home and back to get changed.

1.30pm: We come back to school in old clothes so we can work at gardening or play football. The girls sweep and clean and wash uniforms. Boys do heavier work (but less of it). It's hot.

3.30pm: The handbell rings and we can go home, very tired. Sometimes there's homework, but I usually don't have time because I have to help at home, cleaning or looking after my brothers and sisters.

IT MUST BE HARD WORK!

IN MANY COUNTRIES OF THE SOUTH, SCHOOLS HAVE THEIR OWN GARDEN OR SMALL FARM WHERE PUPILS CAN LEARN ABOUT FARMING AND RAISE MONEY. AGRICULTURE IS AN IMPORTANT SCHOOL SUBJECT.

MAKES YOU THINK

THINGS TO DO

19

WORK AND MONEY

WHAT DO YOU WANT TO BE WHEN YOU GROW UP, ROBERT?

A DEMOLITION EXPERT!

YOU COULD DO THAT ANY-WHERE IN THE WORLD. THERE ARE LOTS OF CITIES IN THE SOUTH. LOOK...

CITIES IN THE SOUTH HAVE BEEN GROWING REALLY FAST. GOVERNMENTS OFTEN CAN'T BUILD ENOUGH ROADS AND HOUSES, SEWERS, POWER AND WATER SUPPLIES FOR THE PEOPLE WHO LIVE THERE.

GUATEMALA CITY

ASMARA

RANGOON

NAIROBI

PHNOM PENH

BANGLADESH

HERE'S A SHANTY TOWN.

IT'S VERY CROWDED. WHY DO PEOPLE LIVE HERE?

THEY OFTEN GET A BETTER JOB AND MORE MONEY IN THE CITY THAN IN THE COUNTRYSIDE.

HOW MANY KINDS OF WORK CAN YOU SEE IN THIS PICTURE?

ANSWERS: FISHERMAN, STALL HOLDER, BUILDER, DOCTOR, BASKET WEAVER, ROAD SWEEPER, TAXI-DRIVER (RICKSHAW).

WHAT SORT OF JOBS DO PEOPLE DO?

WE WORK FOR OURSELVES.

FISHERMAN

MARKET TRADER

WE ALL PAY TAXES.

WE WORK FOR A BOSS.

TEACHER NURSE OFFICE WORKER SHOP WORKER

HOW DO OTHER PEOPLE MANAGE?

THEY FIND DIFFERENT WAYS TO MAKE MONEY.

I RECYCLE RUBBISH I FIND ON TIPS...

...THEN I SELL IT.

I LIVE AND WORK IN MY TAXI IN DELHI.

TAXI

HE HAS HIS MEALS ON WHEELS! BUT HE COULDN'T KEEP A FAMILY IN A TAXI.

WE LIFT...

...CARRY...

BUILD AND REPAIR THINGS.

OFTEN PEOPLE HAVE SEVERAL JOBS.

NEPAL

I GOT UP AT FOUR THIS MORNING, FETCHED WATER, MADE BREAKFAST, FED THE CHICKENS, TOOK THE CHILDREN TO SCHOOL, TOOK THE BABY TO MY SISTER'S, WORKED IN THE SHOP TILL NOON, THEN RUSHED TO THE CANTEEN WHERE I SERVED LUNCH FOR EVERYONE. DIDN'T HAVE TIME TO EAT MYSELF. THEN I WENT TO MY CLEANING JOB IN THE OFFICE, PICKED THE KIDS UP AT FOUR, CAME BACK, BUYING BREAD ON THE WAY, HUNTED FOR EGGS, TOOK THE BABY TO THE CLINIC, WASHED THE CLOTHES, AND NOW I'M CLEANING UP BEFORE DINNER, PUTTING THE KIDS TO BED, AND FETCHING SOME MORE WATER. WHAT A DAY!

BECAUSE I EARN LESS I DON'T HAVE MUCH POWER.

WHAT PEOPLE EARN

22

AMOUNT OF MONEY EARNED BY AN AVERAGE WORKER IN A YEAR AND HOW IT IS SPENT

MANY PEOPLE IN THE SOUTH EARN LESS THAN PEOPLE DO IN THE NORTH, SO THEY SPEND THEIR MONEY IN DIFFERENT WAYS.

LET'S SEE HOW PEOPLE IN FOUR COUNTRIES SPEND WHAT THEY EARN.

THE AVERAGE AMOUNT EARNED BY ONE PERSON IN A YEAR

IN MOZAMBIQUE

IN INDIA

IN COLOMBIA

IN CANADA

MOZAMBIQUE | IN INDIA | IN COLOMBIA | IN CANADA

- FOOD
- EDUCATION
- RENT AND FUEL
- CLOTHES
- TRANSPORT
- OTHER EXPENSES (eg. TAXES)

MAKES YOU THINK

This metal worker is from Burkina Faso in Africa. Many people all over the world do similar work but in different ways, according to where they live and what facilities and resources they have.

THINGS TO DO

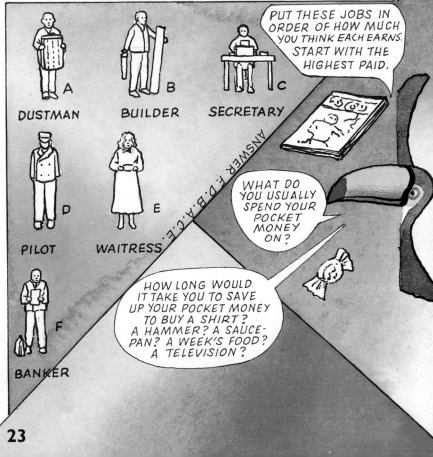

PUT THESE JOBS IN ORDER OF HOW MUCH YOU THINK EACH EARNS. START WITH THE HIGHEST PAID.

A DUSTMAN

B BUILDER

C SECRETARY

D PILOT

E WAITRESS

F BANKER

ANSWER: F.D.B.A.C.E.

WHAT DO YOU USUALLY SPEND YOUR POCKET MONEY ON?

HOW LONG WOULD IT TAKE YOU TO SAVE UP YOUR POCKET MONEY TO BUY A SHIRT? A HAMMER? A SAUCEPAN? A WEEK'S FOOD? A TELEVISION?

23

PLAYTIME

HOW TO MAKE A GOURD RATTLE

"TRY MAKING THIS FOR YOUR OWN FESTIVAL OF MUSIC."

"IN COUNTRIES LIKE NIGERIA AND SIERRA LEONE, RATTLES ARE MADE FROM GOURDS (DRIED, HOLLOW FRUIT— RATHER LIKE A MARROW) OR FROM LEATHER."

YOU'LL NEED:

* A BLOWN-UP BALLOON
* NEWSPAPER
* WALLPAPER PASTE
* A STICK (DOWELLING) OR ROLLED CARDBOARD
* DRIED BEANS
* PAINT
* STRING, FEATHERS AND SHELLS

1. TEAR THE NEWSPAPER INTO STRIPS, SOAK IT IN WALLPAPER PASTE AND USE 8 LAYERS OF IT TO COVER THE BALLOON (THIS IS CALLED PAPIER MACHÉ). LEAVE A SMALL HOLE AT THE END WHERE THE BALLOON IS KNOTTED. MAKE SURE YOU WASH YOUR HANDS AFTER USING THE WALLPAPER PASTE.

2. AFTER THE PASTE HAS DRIED, POP THE BALLOON AND REMOVE IT FROM INSIDE. PUT A HANDFUL OF DRIED BEANS OR SEEDS INTO THE PAPIER MACHÉ SHELL.

3. PUSH THE STICK INTO THE HOLE (OR USE TIGHTLY ROLLED CARDBOARD INSTEAD) AND GLUE IT IN PLACE WITH MORE PAPER AND PASTE.

4. WHEN IT'S DRY, PAINT YOUR RATTLE AND DECORATE IT WITH FEATHERS, STRING AND SHELLS INSTEAD OF THE PAPIER MACHÉ YOU COULD USE AN EMPTY PLASTIC BOTTLE.

MATCH THE GAME TO THE COUNTRY

"SEE HOW MANY OF THESE YOU CAN MATCH TO THE COUNTRY THEY CAME FROM."

"HMMM... IT'S NOT EASY!"

1. CHESS
2. FOOTBALL
3. TENNIS
4. POLO
5. JUDO
6. LACROSSE
7. DOLLS
8. DICE

A. NORTH AMERICA
B. INDIA
C. IRAN
D. EGYPT
E. CHINA
F. JAPAN
G. FRANCE
H. EVERYWHERE

1B, 2E, 3G, 4C, 5F, 6A, 7H, 8D.

25

DOLLS AROUND THE WORLD

CHILDREN EVERY-WHERE PLAY WITH DOLLS. YOU CAN MAKE YOUR OWN, USING CLAY OR PLAY DOUGH; GIVE THEM HAPPY OR SAD FACES.

TRY COPYING THIS ONE. PAINT THEM, OR DRESS THEM USING OFF-CUTS OF FABRIC OR BITS OF RIBBON.

WORRY DOLLS

I COME FROM GUATEMALA IN SOUTH AMERICA AND WE PLAY WITH WORRY DOLLS LIKE THESE. WE KEEP THE DOLLS IN A BOX BY THE BED.

YOU'RE ONLY ALLOWED SIX DOLLS, SO YOU'RE ONLY ALLOWED SIX PROBLEMS! WHILE YOU'RE SLEEPING THE DOLLS WILL TRY TO SOLVE YOUR PROBLEMS FOR YOU.

WHAT A WONDERFUL IDEA!

IF WE HAVE A WORRY ON OUR MINDS BEFORE WE GO TO SLEEP WE TAKE THE DOLLS OUT OF THE BOX AND TELL THEM OUR PROBLEMS, ONE PROBLEM FOR EACH DOLL.

HOW TO MAKE THEM

YOU'LL NEED:

* PIPE CLEANERS

* COLOURED COTTON OR WOOL

* THICK FUSE WIRE

* A PEN

* MASKING TAPE

* SCISSORS (BE CAREFUL USING THESE)

THE DOLLS ARE ONLY 2 CENTIMETRES HIGH, SO WORK SMALL!

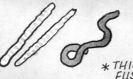

MAKE A FIGURE BY TWISTING TWO SHORT PIECES OF THE FUSE WIRE ROUND A 2-CENTIMETRE LENGTH OF PIPE CLEANER, TO MAKE ARMS AND LEGS.

USE A SMALL PIECE OF MASKING TAPE TO MAKE THE HEAD—YOU CAN DRAW A FACE ON IT.

WRAP THE WOOL AND/OR COTTON ROUND THE BODY AND LIMBS TO MAKE DIFFERENT COLOURED CLOTHES. YOU CAN STICK SOME WOOL ON THE HEAD FOR HAIR.

I'M MAKING SIX DIFFERENT ONES TO KEEP IN A LITTLE BOX BESIDE MY BED.

GAMES FROM AROUND THE WORLD

NIGER

FIVE FIELD KONO – FROM KOREA

EACH PLAYER HAS SEVEN PIECES AND CAN ONLY MOVE DIAGONALLY. NO JUMPING OR TAKING PIECES! THE FIRST TO GET ALL THEIR PIECES TO THE OTHER SIDE WINS.

IT'S HARDER THAN IT LOOKS...

EAGLE – FROM MALAWI

THIS ONE'S FOR THE PLAYGROUND. YOU NEED A GROUP OF FRIENDS TO PLAY WITH.

ONE CHILD IS THE EAGLE AND ALL THE OTHERS ARE CHICKENS. THE CHICKENS ALL STAND IN A GROUP FACING THE EAGLE AND ARE SEPARATED FROM HIM BY A LINE. THE EAGLE WANTS TO EAT THE CHICKENS! THEY MUST TRY TO CROSS THE LINE WITHOUT GETTING CAUGHT. WHEN THE EAGLE TOUCHES THEM, THEY JOIN HIS TEAM.

MAKES YOU THINK

THERE ARE SO MANY DIFFERENT KINDS OF PEOPLE IN THE WORLD. WOULDN'T IT BE BORING IF EVERYONE WAS THE SAME?

BUT WE'VE GOT MORE IN COMMON THAN WE HAVE DIFFERENCES. THAT'S ALL PART OF HOW THE WORLD WORKS!

THE **MAKES YOU THINK** GAME

GLOSSARY

Aid Money, food or equipment sent to poor countries by governments or other organisations in rich countries.

Cash Crop A plant like rubber, cocoa or tobacco, grown as a raw material in the South to sell to other countries, often in the North. Cash crops earn money that is used for paying off the debt that countries in the South owe to the North.

Cocoyam Root vegetable.

Colonies Countries which are part of an empire ruled by another country.

Debt Money owed to someone.

Distribute Share out.

Emergency Aid Aid sent to countries where there has been a natural disaster or famine.

Employer Someone who pays you to work for them.

Environment The air, water, land, buildings, animal and plant life all around us.

Export To send produce like cash crops out of the country, as part of trade.

Famine A time when there's not enough food to feed everyone and people are dying of hunger and disease.

Food Mountain When more food is grown than people can afford or want to buy, it is stored. This store is called a 'food mountain'.

Foreign Debts Another name for the North-South Debt. Also, any debt owed by one country to another.

Manufactured Goods Things made by people from natural resources, for example tables, cars, paper and chocolate.

Natural Disasters Earthquakes, floods, storms, tidal waves and volcanoes erupting; any disaster not caused by people's actions. Some of these, like droughts and floods, can be made worse by humans not looking after the environment properly.

Natural Resource Anything natural that can be turned into something people want to buy or use, such as coal, oil, gas, gold, iron, forests (for wood) and good soil for farming. People are a natural resource, too.

The North A word for the rich countries (also called the West or First World), usually Europe, North America, Japan, Australia and New Zealand.

North-South Debt The money owed by the poor countries to the rich countries.

Official Work A way of describing jobs done for an employer. Official workers pay tax.

Plantain A vegetable that looks like a large, green banana.

Quinoa A grain-like vegetable, similar to millet.

Raw Materials Natural resources used for manufactured goods.

Rent Money paid to someone (a landlord) who owns your house or land.

Shanty Town A group of shelters made of old wood, corrugated iron and anything else that can be found. They have no sewers, water or electricity and are often found at the edges of big cities in the South.

The South A word for the poor countries (also called the Developing World or Third World), mainly the countries of Africa, Central and South America, the Caribbean, the Indian subcontinent and Asia (except Japan).

Tax Money paid to the government by people working for an employer. Governments use tax money to build roads, schools, hospitals and so on.

Trade The buying and selling of raw materials, produce and manufactured goods. Countries buy these things from and sell them to each other.

Yam Root vegetable.

ABOUT OXFAM

Now you have some idea of how the world works. You can share what you know with other people. You can join with **Oxfam**, working for a fairer world.

Every day, millions of people in the countries of the South go without the things we take for granted in the North: food, shelter, water, education, health care and the right to make decisions about our lives. For many people, things are getting worse, not better. **Oxfam** helps people break out of their poverty, supporting them as they make changes that will last.

The early years

In 1942, the world was at war. In Oxford people formed the Oxford Committee for Famine Relief. Its aim: to help people in Greece, where women and children were hungry, and to campaign for food and medicines to be allowed into Greece. The campaign was partly successful and some food got through. When peace came in 1945, the Oxford Committee found that there was still work to be done. It raised money and collected clothing for refugees in Europe. In 1965 the organisation took the name **Oxfam**.

Oxfam overseas

Today **Oxfam** works in 77 countries. Much of its work is in places where conflict makes life terrible for innocent victims. While emergency relief is an important part of **Oxfam's** work, it also cares about more lasting relief of suffering. It works with poor people as they find ways to break free of sickness, illiteracy and poverty and to question the unfairness that keeps them poor. Many self-help projects only need a little money to get off the ground. About a third of **Oxfam** grants are for less than £3,000 but these small sums can have a big impact. You have read about some of the things that make life difficult for people in the South, and how people cope. Here are some projects **Oxfam** has supported: • buying BookBoxes for schools in Namibia • supporting school gardens in Tanzania • funding a puppet theatre which puts on performances about health in Rajasthan • providing transport and equipment for community radio in Brazil.

Oxfam in the UK and Ireland

In 1942 the Oxford Committee campaigned to get aid to Greece. **Oxfam** still campaigns and tries to tell people and governments what can be done to help poor people tackle poverty and unfairness and **Oxfam** also works in schools. *HOW THE WORLD WORKS* is a part of this programme. **Oxfam** also means 'shops'. There are over 850 **Oxfam** shops, and you may have bought this book from one of them. The **Oxfam** catalogue is crammed with 'fair trade' goods. **Oxfam** started most of the fund-raising ideas that are so common now.

Working for a fairer world

Since 1942 **Oxfam** has spread across the world, giving support to people, no matter what their race, colour, gender, politics or religion. This support comes in many ways: for a woman who can get safe drinking water from a new well in her village; as shelter and support for a refugee; by someone who is prepared to listen to your problems; through two meals a day for a family instead of one because of better farming methods. **Oxfam** gives an opportunity for everyone to make this support possible, to make our world a fairer place.

To find out more about **Oxfam**, write to us:
in England: *Oxfam, Anniversary Information, 274 Banbury Road, Oxford OX2 7DZ*
in Northern Ireland: *Oxfam, PO Box 70, 52-4 Dublin Road, Belfast BT2 7HN*
in Ireland: *Oxfam, 202 Lower Rathmines Road, Dublin 6*
in Scotland: *Oxfam, Floor 5, Fleming House, Renfrew Street, Glasgow G3 3T*
in Wales: *Oxfam, 46-8 Station Road, Llanishen, Cardiff CF4 5LU*
in Australia: *Community Aid Abroad, 156 George Street, Fitzroy, Victoria 3065*
in Belgium: *Oxfam Belgique, 39 rue de Conseil, 1050 Bruxelles*
in Canada: *Oxfam Canada, 251 Laurier Avenue W, Room 301, Ottawa, Ontario KIP 5J6*
in Hong Kong: *Oxfam, Ground Floor - 3B, June Garden, 28 Tung Chau Street, Tai Kok Tsui, Kowloon*
in Quebec: *Oxfam Quebec, 169 rue St Paul est, Montreal 127, Quebec H2Y 1G8*
in the USA: *Oxfam America, 115 Broadway, Boston, Massachusetts 02116*

INDEX

Copyright © Oxfam Activities Ltd 1992
Illustrations © Two-Can Publishing 1992

This edition first published in Great Britain in 1992 by
Two-Can Publishing Ltd
346 Old Street
London EC1V 9NQ
in association with Scholastic Publications Ltd

Printed by Amadeus in Rome, Italy.

10 9 8 7 6 5 4 3 2 1

(Pbk) ISBN: 1-85434-201-0
(Hbk) ISBN: 1-85434-202-9

Photograph Credits:
p.2 J. Hartley p.3 B.J. Knapp p.7 B. Pratt, M. Goldwater, J. Hartley, Oxfam p.8 A. Couldridge, J. Hartley, A.C. Gonzales p.10 P. Jackson p.12 J. Hartley p.13 C. Johnson p.15 N. Southern p.16 G. Poole, Oxfam, J. Hartley p.18 A. Couldridge p.20 A.C. Gonzales, W. Holt, J. Davis, B. Beardwood, M. Goldwater, J. Alderson p.22 J. Hartley p.23 J. Hartley p.24 F. Rubin p.27 Oxfam Cover photo M. Thompson Back cover photo J. Hartley. All photographs reproduced courtesy of Oxfam.

All illustrations by Aidan Potts

The author and publishers would like to thank the staff and 9 to 10 year old pupils at Kingswood School in Lambeth, London,
the World Development Movement and the Oxfam Development Education Unit.